DEPARTMENT OF THE NAVY
HEADQUARTERS UNITED STATES MARINE CORPS
2 NAVY ANNEX
WASHINGTON, DC 20380–1775

I0430069

MCO P4450.7E
LPP-2
25 May 94

MARINE CORPS ORDER P4450.7E

From: Commandant of the Marine Corps
To: Distribution List

Subj: MARINE CORPS WAREHOUSING MANUAL

Encl: (1) LOCATOR SHEET

Reports Required: I. Storage Space Utilization and Occupancy
                       Report (Report Symbol DD-4450-02),
                       par. 4000.2
                   II. Individual Storage Unit Report (Report
                       Symbol DD-4450-03) par. 4002.1

1. <u>Purpose</u>. To consolidate, revise, and standardize the procedures to be used by Marine Corps activities in the storage and warehousing of supplies within the Marine Corps.

2. <u>Cancellation</u>. MCO P4450.7D.

3. <u>Summary of Revision</u>. This revision includes a new stock locator system for deployable units. It also places procedures for field warehousing in a separate chapter.

4. <u>Action</u>. The procedures outlined in this Manual are to be implemented as soon as possible.

5. <u>Recommendations</u>. Recommendations concerning the contents of the Marine Corps Warehousing Manual are invited and should be submitted to the Commandant of the Marine Corps (LPP-2) via the appropriate chain of command.

6. <u>Reserve Applicability</u>. This Manual is applicable to the Marine Corps Reserve.

7. Certification. Reviewed and approved this date.

R. A. TIEBOUT
Deputy Chief of Staff
for Installations and Logistics

DISTRIBUTION: PCN 10205620000

    Copy to: 7000110 (55)
              7000093/8145005 (2)
              7000099, 144 (1)
              8145001 (1)

MCO P4450.7E
25 May 94

LOCATOR SHEET

Subject: MARINE CORPS WAREHOUSING MANUAL

Location: _____

(Indicate the location(s) of the copy(ies) of this
publication.)

MARINE CORPS WAREHOUSING MANUAL

RECORD OF CHANGES

Log completed change action, as indicated.

Change Number	Date of Change	Date Entered	Signature of Person Incorporated Change

CONTENTS

CHAPTER

    1   GENERAL INFORMATION

    2   WAREHOUSE OPERATIONS

    3   FIELD WAREHOUSING

    4   REPORTS

    5   WAREHOUSING REFERENCES

APPENDIX

    A   GLOSSARY OF TERMS

    B   STORAGE LOCATION EXAMPLES

    C   STORAGE CONTAINERS

    D   ACRONYMS AND ABBREVIATIONS

MARINE CORPS WAREHOUSING MANUAL

CHAPTER 1

GENERAL INFORMATION

	PARAGRAPH	PAGE
INTRODUCTION	1000	1-3
SCOPE	1001	1-3
RESPONSIBILITIES OF WAREHOUSING OFFICERS . .	1002	1-3

MARINE CORPS WAREHOUSING MANUAL

CHAPTER 1

GENERAL INFORMATION

1000. <u>INTRODUCTION</u>

1. <u>Purpose</u>. The primary purpose of this Manual is to provide
instructions and procedures whereby the Marine Corps Warehousing
Program may be administered per policies established by the
Department of Defense (DOD), Secretary of the Navy, Commandant of
the Marine Corps (CMC), and various joint service directives. For
a glossary of terms, see appendix A.

2. <u>Applicability</u>. The instructions contained herein are
applicable to all Marine Corps activities performing storage and
warehousing services.

1001. <u>SCOPE</u>. The instructions contained herein provide Marine
Corps policy and procedures to be followed in establishing, using,
expanding, inactivating, and disestablishing storage and
warehousing operations; cross-servicing of warehousing by and among
DOD components, and between DoD components and Federal Government
agencies; assuring the most effective, economical use of storage
assets; providing a means for greater flexibility in the
positioning of stocks owned by the Marine Corps; disestablishing
and inactivating facilities; and warehousing and rewarehousing of
materiel within the Marine Corps.

1002. <u>RESPONSIBILITIES OF WAREHOUSING OFFICERS</u>

1. <u>General</u>. Personnel assigned the responsibility as a
warehousing officer must provide the management necessary to ensure
the maximum utilization of storage and warehousing facilities as
stated in DOD 4145.19-R-1.

2. <u>Responsibilities</u>. Warehousing officers are responsible for the
following:

    a. Management of the receiving, inspecting, storing, issuing, and shipping of supplies and equipment.

    b. Preservation, packaging, and packing (PP&P) of all classes
and categories of supplies and equipment except class III (bulk
fuel) and class V (ammunition).

    c. Care of equipment and supplies while in storage.

    d. Development of planographs and the supervision of the
layout of covered and open storage space.

    e. Effective and efficient utilization of storage space,
including use of square and cubic feet of facilities designated for
storage use.

    f. Supervision of storage space utilization and occupancy
reporting, and individual storage unit reporting.

    g. Knowledgeable of policies and procedures for cross-service
agreements for space, facilities, and warehousing services.

    h. Determination of requirements, control of the
allocation, and utilization of materiels handling equipment,
conveyors, automatic materiels handling systems, storage aids, and
equipment for PP&P.

    i. Supervision of proper work methods and improvement of
methods on a continuing basis.

    j. Understanding the principles and application of work
measurement programs or systems.

    k. Development of warehousing modernization efforts per
MCO 4450.10.

    l. Supervision of warehousing administration.

    m. Stock management, data processing, and management
engineering procedures as applied to storage operations.

    n. Understanding the principles and applications of logistics
marking and reading symbology (LOGMARS) and other warehousing
support systems.

MARINE CORPS WAREHOUSING MANUAL

CHAPTER 2

WAREHOUSE OPERATIONS

	PARAGRAPH	PAGE
SCOPE	2000	2-3
INTRODUCTION	2001	2-3
STORAGE CATEGORIES	2002	2-3
WAREHOUSING CONTAINERS	2003	2-4
STORAGE LAYOUT	2004	2-4
STOCK LOCATION	2005	2-4
STOCK LOCATION FILE	2006	2-7
MARKING OF STORAGE COMPLEX/CONTAINERS	2007	2-7
MISCELLANEOUS	2008	2-9

FIGURE

2-1	FMF WAREHOUSE CONTROL CARD (FORM NAVMC 10849)	2-11

MARINE CORPS WAREHOUSING MANUAL

CHAPTER 2

WAREHOUSE OPERATIONS

2000. SCOPE. Warehousing and storage operations include, but are not, limited to, the unloading, checking, sorting, and placing in storage; withdrawing from storage, checking, and loading; using storage space; inspecting stored materiel; PP&P and other care of materiel; physical inventory and special security measures, when specifically requested; and documentation incident to the aforementioned services.

2001. INTRODUCTION

1. General. The maintenance of stocks in a good state of readiness requires that such supplies be preserved, packaged, packed, and located in such a manner as to permit expeditious handling. Further, materiel should be packed and marked to permit its rapid, orderly access with a minimum of confusion and loss of materiel. Constant care must be taken to ensure that supplies are maintained in a current and serviceable condition.

2. Supplies Maintained in Garrison. When organic supplies are maintained in garrison, they shall be inspected, as required, to ensure serviceability, adequacy of preservation, and/or proper identification. Such supplies should be stored to allow for ready access, in stock maintenance, stock rotation, and/or inventory.

3. Deployment. Upon receipt of a deployment order, supplies shall

be inspected to ensure completeness of tactical and location markings. FMFM 4-1 provides guidelines for the conduct of field operations.

2002. STORAGE CATEGORIES

1. General Information. Warehousing is divided into three major categories of storage: bin, medium, and bulk. Such categories are based upon the popularity, physical characteristics, and stock level of supplies.

2. Bin Storage. Bin storage is designed primarily to accommodate small, rapid moving items, such as repair parts, handtools, and hardware.

3. Medium Storage. Medium storage locations are those locations designed to accommodate items which bare too large by either size or quantity for bin storage but not large enough to warrant being placed into an individual storage container.

4. Bulk Storage. A bulk storage location consists of those items which by either size or quantity warrant being placed in an individual storage container.

2003. WAREHOUSING CONTAINERS. The type of container used in warehousing shall be dictated by the materiel which is being stored. The storage containers shown in appendixes B and C are available for use.

2004. STORAGE LAYOUT

1. General. Per NAVSUP Pub. 529, the layout of storage space and facilities should:

   a. Be sufficiently versatile to meet all storage situations.

   b. Be fully responsive to mechanized materiel handling.

   c. Meet every requirement of computer processing of documentation which affects receipt, storage, and issue of supplies.

   d. Facilitate effective space management.

   e. Provide a pattern which is compatible with efficient work methods for storing and withdrawing stocks.

2. Responsibilities. All Marine Corps activities maintaining storage and warehouse facilities will use the stock location systems prescribed herein. Each activity will determine the area and station assignment necessary for its particular operation and issue supplementary instructions regarding the same.

2005. STOCK LOCATION

1. General. Proper stock locations are essential to effective warehousing. Stock location numbers and files must be established and maintained in such a manner to permit rapid location of supplies both in garrison and deployed environments.

2. Physical Location Codes. The physical location code is a part of the item locator file and is used to physically identify each individual storage location. There are two stock location numbering systems used within the Marine Corps: the nondeployable unit and the deployable unit locator systems. The nondeployable system will be used by nondeploying units and units which normally do not deploy as a complete entity (deploy in blocks; i.e., Supported Activities Supply System (SASSY) management units, etc.). The deployable locator system will be used by all other units.

3. Nondeployable Locator System. The nondeployable stock location system consists of nine characters, alpha and numeric combinations, as follows:

    a. Area/First Position/Alpha. The first character is alpha and may represent a group of buildings within a complex, an open storage area, a single building or a warehouse, a shed, or a floor when utilizing a multistory warehouse.

    b. Station/Second and Third Positions/Numeric. The second and third characters are numeric and are used to identify a station within an area. These digits may be used to identify stock picking stations, stations receipt of materiel for stowing, packing stations, floors of building, sections of a warehouse, or a building within an area. Collection, assembly, or dropoff stations in a mechanized warehouse system may also be identified.

    c. Aisle or Row/Fourth and Fifth Positions/Numeric. The fourth and fifth characters are numeric and are used to identify aisles or rows within a station. An individual numbering system is used within each station.

    d. Segment/Sixth and Seventh Positions/Numeric. The sixth and seventh characters are numeric and are used to identify segments of an aisle, row, or container. A segment may be short lot, stack, rack, or bin or a vertical apportionment thereof. Within an aisle, the odd numbers will be on the left; and the even numbers will be on the right (based on the direction of flow as related to transportation or main aisles/roadways).

   e. Level/Eighth Position/Alpha. The eighth character is alpha and represents the level within segments/containers. Where not applicable, such as in bulk storage, the letter "A" will be assigned.

   f. Compartment/Ninth Position/Alpha. The ninth character is alpha and identifies a subdivision of the level within the segment, such as a drawer or compartment of a roto bin. Where not applicable, such as in bulk storage, the letter "A" will be assigned.

   NOTE: Criteria for the sequential assignment of an aisle or row and segment designator is critical since it determines the amount of physical movement required in receipt, stowing, and stock picking operations. The assignment of locations must provide for orderly work performance without returning to an area previously transversed. Location positions six through nine only shall be used in the marking of inserts. See appendix B.

4. Deployable Unit Location System

   a. The deployable unit location system was designed to provide the unit with as much flexibility as possible. The stock location number consists of nine alpha/numeric digits as outlined herein.

   (1) Embark, Serial, and Tactical Markings/First Fours Positions/Alpha/Numeric. The first four characters may be alpha/numeric depending on the unit's needs. These positions should be used primarily for embarkation numbers, serial numbers, and tactical markings; however, they may be used for other purposes, as required. These positions could be used to identify buildings/dumps or in conjunction with positions five through seven to expand box number availability. The unit must identify in writing how these positions are being used. It is recommended that these positions be controlled at the major subordinate command level.

   (2) Type of Storage/Fifth Position/Numeric. The fifth character is numeric and is used to identify the type of storage. If equipment is located by type of storage, this position can be used in conjunction with positions six and seven to expand

the range of box numbers from 99 to 297.

        (3) <u>Box or Container/Sixth and Seventh Positions/Numeric</u>. The sixth and seventh characters are numeric and are used to identify the box or container number.

        (4) <u>Level/Eighth Position/Alpha</u>. The eighth character is alpha and represents the level within the container. Where not applicable, such as in bulk containers, the letter "A" will be assigned.

        (5) <u>Compartment/Ninth Position/Alpha</u>. The ninth character is alpha and identifies a subdivision of the level within the containers. Where not applicable, such as in bulk containers, the letter "A" will be assigned.

2-6

   b. The following is a sample of embarkation/serial number/unit tactical markings:

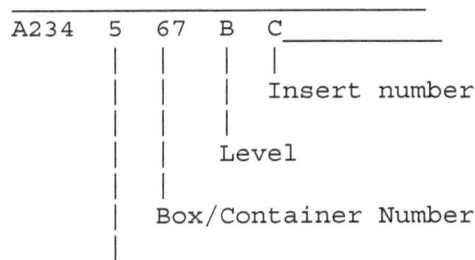

```
A234  5  67  B  C_____
       |  |   |  |
       |  |   |  Insert number
       |  |   |
       |  |   Level
       |  |
       |  Box/Container Number
       |
       Type of Storage:  (1) Bin Storage Unit
                         (2) Medium Storage Unit
                         (3) Bulk Storage
                         (4) Vehicles
                         (5) through (9) As Required
                             Locally
```

2006. <u>STOCK LOCATION FILE</u>

1. <u>General Information</u>. Flexibility is of primary importance in maintaining stock locator records within the using units. To maintain such flexibility, it is mandatory that local commanders use a stock locator system. The three systems available for use within the Marine Corps are manual, automated data processing equipment end user computer equipment (EUCE), and mainframe

computer programs.

2. <u>Manual</u>. An FMF Warehouse Control Card (form NAVMC 10849) shall be used to maintain a manual-mechanical locator stock location system (see figure 2-1).

3. <u>EUCE</u>. Personal computers have the capability of providing a mechanized stock locator file. The Asset Tracking for Logistics and Supply System (ATLASS) possesses this capability. This system can be used in both garrison and field environments using guidance contained in UM 4400-120.

4. <u>Mainframe Computer Support</u>. Mainframe computer support has the capability of providing a stock locator file which can be updated on an as-required basis. These programs can be used in both garrison and field environments.

2007.   <u>MARKING OF STORAGE COMPLEX/CONTAINERS</u>

1. <u>General Information</u>. The standard markings of the storage complex and containers are essential for the rapid and orderly

assembly and location of supplies. The following general rules will be followed in the marking of the storage complex and container:

   a. <u>Nondeployable Location System</u>

     (1) <u>Enclosed/Improved Storage</u>. Markings will be made with suitable traffic paint on floors or paving, or enamel on signs or placards.

       (a) <u>Area</u>. Each building and storage lot will be marked with a 6-inch letter adjacent to their traffic entrance, indicating its assigned area.

       (b) <u>Station</u>. At the intersection of stations, floor marking or signs will be posted which indicate the area and station. Within stations of sufficient size to require further markings, the area and station will be indicated at the intersection of transportation/traffic aisles and rows.

       (c) <u>Aisle/Row</u>. Aisle/row numbers will be painted on the floor or signs in such a manner that they will be readily visible to a person entering the row from either direction.

       (d) <u>Segment</u>. The segment number will be painted in

such a manner that it will be readily visible when standing in front of the segment and will be placed so that the number is centered on the segment to which it applies.

       (e) <u>Level</u>. Bins and racks will have the level painted in the center of the shelf or crossmember and will indicate that the supplies placed thereon are at that level; i.e., the level will never be interpreted to apply to supplies stored below the level marking.

       (f) <u>Compartment</u>. Compartments will be marked from left to right within the level when facing the segment. (See appendix B.)

    (2) <u>Unimproved Storage</u>. Unimproved storage will be marked in the same basic manner; however, stakes and placards will bemused rather than floor markings.

  b. <u>Deployable Location System</u>

    (1) <u>General Information</u>. The markings, as outlined in paragraph 2007.1b(3), following, are those tactical markings required by the Fleet Marine Force (FMF).

    (2) <u>Area</u>. If more than one storage complex is used, each building and storage lot will be marked with a 6-inch letter adjacent to the traffic entrance, indicating its assigned area.

2-8

    (3) <u>Marking Containers</u>

       (a) <u>Bin Unit Markings</u>. The location markings shall be placed on the container as shown in appendixes B and C. The lettering shall be in 1-inch black block letters on the containers and 1/2-inch-high yellow or white block lettering on the inserts.

       (b) <u>Medium/Bulk Storage Containers</u>. Medium and bulk containers shall be marked as indicated in appendixes B and C. The location markings shall be in 3-inch-high black block lettering.

2. <u>Responsibility</u>. Each activity will be responsible for ensuring that markings used are consistent throughout the entire storage complex and that warehousemen/stockmen are thoroughly knowledgeable on the marking system used. New employees/arrivals will be schooled on the activity's marking system.

2008. <u>MISCELLANEOUS</u>

1. <u>Preservation and Packing</u>. All items shall be afforded the degree of protection required to assure serviceability at the using

unit. All items which are susceptible to corrosion and deterioration shall be preserved and packaged to conform to the Level A requirements as outlined in MCO P4030.36 and will be subsequently stored in field warehousing containers without destroying the integrity of the Level A protection.

2. _Shelf Life_. Shelf life items are those items of supply possessing deteriorative or unstable characteristics to the degree that a storage time period must be assigned. These items require intensified management per DOD 4140.27-M to minimize losses to the Government.

3. _Hazardous Material_. Hazardous material consists of explosives, flammables, corrosives, and radioactive materials which, because of their nature, present real or potential hazards to life and/or property and require special storage. The procedures for the storage of hazardous material are outlined in MCO 4450.12.

4. _LOGMARS_. The logistical application of bar-coded technology within the Marine Corps provides an automated means to more efficiently manage storage operations.

    a. The Warehouse Support System (WSS) consists of three major functions:

        (1) _Location Determination_. This function allows all incoming supplies to be identified for existing locations.

        (2) _Location Surveillance (Location Verification)_. This function allows the storage officer to validate existing locations.

        (3) _Physical Inventory_. This function provides the mechanism to conduct an inventory.

    b. _Systems Requirements_. WSS takes advantage of the portability of personal computer and bar code technology to automate basic warehouse functions. A typical WSS consists of one master unit, several "slave" units (depending on the size of the warehouse), scanning devices, and a telecommunications/radio frequency link to a host mainframe computer. While the system is not designed to be deployable, slave and master units can be relocated within the warehouse with proper support equipment.

    c. Procedures for the implementation of the WSS are contained in UM 4400-171.

MARINE CORPS WAREHOUSING MANUAL

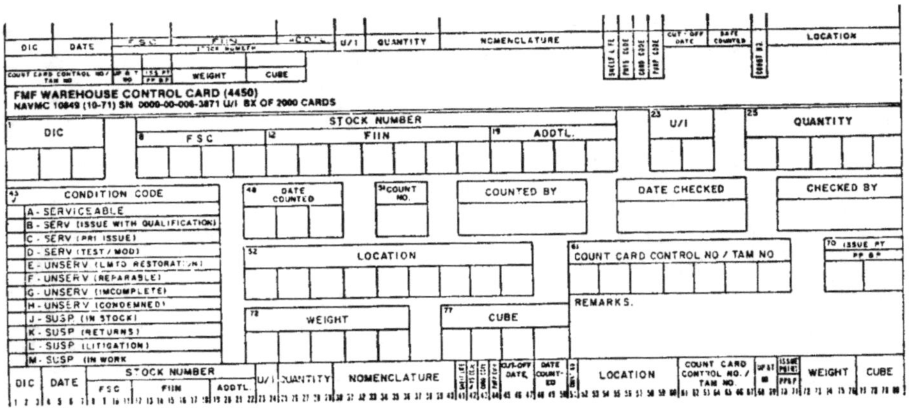

Legend

CC's	Entry
1-3	Enter the document identifier code (DIC), if applicable.
4-7	Enter the Julian date on which the card is prepared.
8-18 1/	Enter the national stock number (NSN) of item and/or location, inventory, or information from the unit personnel and tonnage table (UP&TT), as appropriate.
19-22 1/	Enter additional portion of the NSN or DoD ammunition code (DoDAC) for ammunition.
23-24 1/	Enter the unit of issue for the NSN and/or information from the UP&TT, as appropriate.
25-29	Enter the quantity of the item being counted or quantity of the item on location, and/or information from the UP&TT, as appropriate.
30-40 1/	Enter the brief noun nomenclature of the item and/or information from the UP&TT, as appropriate.

Figure 2-1.--FMF Warehouse Control Card (Form NAVMC 10849).

Figure 2-1.--FMF Warehouse Control Card (Form 10849).

MARINE CORPS WAREHOUSING MANUAL

CC's	Entry
41	Enter the appropriate shelf life of the item.
42	Enter the appropriate physical security code of the item.
43	Enter the appropriate condition code of the item.
44	Enter the appropriate purpose code of the item.
45-47	Enter the number of transactions ceased for inventory, as appropriate.
48-50	Enter the date the inventory count was completed.
51	Enter the count number.
52-60 1/	Enter the location of the item per the appropriate paragraph of this Manual and/or add locator, inventory, and information from the UP&TT, as appropriate.
61-67	Enter the count card control number for inventory count or table of authorized materiel control number (TAMCN), and/or add inventory, as appropriate.
68-69	Enter the applicable UP&TT number for embarkation purposes and/or use for locator and inventory, as appropriate.
70-71	Enter the issue point number, if applicable, or enter in CC 70 the level of protection provided the basic NSN. This level of protection is normally printed on the outer surface of the box, container, or bag in which the item is packaged. If the item is bare (no protection), enter "0." Enter in CC 71 the level of protection of the outer container; e.g., a binnable item in an air-tight envelope container (Level A) placed in a bin location of a 4.2 cube box with a water barrier material (Level A) would read "AA" in CC's 70-71. Also, add locator, inventory, and information from the UP and TT, as appropriate.

Figure 2-1.--FMF Warehouse Control Card (Form NAVMC 10849)--
Continued.

CC's	Entry

72-76   Enter the weight of the container or weight of the
          vehicle.

   NOTE: Binnable or medium bulk items would not have the
          information entered, but a container header for all
          NSNs inside the outer container would have the
          information entered for that box. Also, add
          inventory, as appropriate.

77-80   Enter the cube of the container or vehicle. The same
          note applies to binnable and medium bulk material.
          Also, add inventory, as appropriate.

1/ Required entry.

          Figure 2-1.--FMF Warehouse Control Card (Form NAVMC 10849)--
                       Continued.

MARINE CORPS WAREHOUSING MANUAL

CHAPTER 3

FIELD WAREHOUSING

	PARAGRAPH	PAGE
FIELD STORAGE LOCATION	3000	3-3
AREA SELECTION	3001	3-3
SUPPLY DUMP LAYOUT	3002	3-4
PROTECTION FROM THE ELEMENTS	3003	3-4

FIGURE

| 3-1 | TYPICAL ROADSIDE DUMP . . . . | 3-6 |
| 3-2 | TYPICAL DEPTH-STORAGE LAYOUT . . . . | 3-7 |

MARINE CORPS WAREHOUSING MANUAL

CHAPTER 3

FIELD WAREHOUSING

3000. <u>FIELD STORAGE LOCATION</u>. The rapid processing of supplies and equipment from rear areas into advanced supply dumps is essential to close supply support. The problems encountered in the establishment of a field supply dump can be greatly minimized through advanced planning. The information provided herein provides recommended procedures which are considered to be fundamental to field storage operations.

3001. <u>AREA SELECTION</u>. The selection of an area is of major importance in the establishment of a field supply dump. In this respect, the following factors should be given careful consideration:

1. <u>Terrain</u>. Good, all-weather characteristics should be present so as not to interrupt storage operations during inclement weather. Potential storage areas should be adequately drained, sufficiently level to sustain operations, and accessible under all weather conditions. An ideal location would be one which contains a thin layer of topsoil with a hard substrata of coral, sandstone rock, or gravel. Such a location would effectively support the weight of supplies and the wear of heavy traffic. Organic clay and silt soil locations are least desirable and should, if possible, be avoided.

2. <u>Cover</u>. Every advantage should be taken to utilize all available natural cover. Discretion should be used in the selection of isolated wooden areas as potential storage areas, inasmuch as they provide excellent targets for enemy aircraft and/or artillery.

3. <u>Access Roads</u>. Access roads to potential storage sites should be capable of withstanding heavy traffic, regardless of weather conditions. Alternate access roads are desirable and extremely important in that traffic on a main supply route (MSR) may become congested or otherwise disrupted, thereby necessitating the use of another road for accessibility to supplies.

4. <u>Fire Protection</u>. Fire protection devices, such as fire barrels, buckets, fire extinguishers, and handtools, should be

located in a readily accessible area in order to reduce fire loses to a minimum.

5. Size/Security. The size of a potential storage area should be large enough to fulfill the necessary storage requirements but not so large as to render it incapable of being defended from light enemy attacks or infiltration.

6. Location

   a. Primary. The primary field storage location should be centrally located in relation to the supported units and resupply points. The central location of the primary position should allow for maximum support to the using unit.

   b. Alternative. An alternative location should always be selected for use in the event that the primary location cannot be occupied. The alternative location may also be used for the storage of overflow from the primary location.

3002. SUPPLY DUMP LAYOUT

1. General Information. A field supply dump layout is an overlay of the storage area which outlines the location of all supplies and facilities, traffic control points, direction of traffic, and relationship of the forward edge of the battle area (FEBA).

2. Types of Layouts. There are basically two types of field dump supply layouts: roadside and depth-storage. The use of such layouts shall be based upon factors, such as the unit's mission, terrain, road accessibility, and climate. Because of the variable factors which might apply, it is not the intent to prescribe a specific layout which will be appropriate to all situations; rather, it is intended to utilize basic layouts which may be used or modified, as appropriate, to fit any given situation.

   a. Roadside Dump. Figure 3-1 outlines a typical roadside dump. This outline is intended to be used only as a guide in establishing a roadside dump. It contains the essential storage locations and elements which must be considered in the establishment of such a dump.

   b. Depth-Storage Dump. The depth-storage dump is considered standard for use by supply support units of a Marine expeditionary force. In establishing a depth-storage dump, primary considerations should be given to the availability to secondary access roads. Figure 3-2 contains a typical depth-storage dump.

3003. PROTECTION FROM THE ELEMENTS

1. General Information. The three fundamental principles which must be observed in the protection of supplies from the elements are adequate storage shelter, dunnage, and ventilation.

2. Adequate Shelter. Adequate storage shelters may be realized through a number of means including, but not limited to, existing

buildings, tents, tarpaulins, and/or caves. Some of the considerations in selecting such means of shelter are as follows:

   a. Existing Buildings. Existing buildings provide an excellent means of shelter. However, prior to use, such buildings should be inspected for structural adequacy and cleared of such things as flammable or otherwise dangerous materials and debris.

   b. Caves. Caves also afford excellent protection for supplies. However, care must be taken to ensure that caves are reasonably dry and free from moisture seepage and have adequate ventilation.

3. Dunnage. The storage stacks must be raised off the ground by the use of a suitable dunnage material to ensure adequate ventilation is afforded to the materiel. The amount and type of dunnage used shall be dictated by the type of texture of the soil on which the supplies will be placed and the climatic conditions.

4. Ventilation. Material should be stacked in such a manner as to allow 2 feet of airspace between the top of the stack and the cover and to allow for free circulation of air around and between storage containers.

MARINE CORPS WAREHOUSING MANUAL

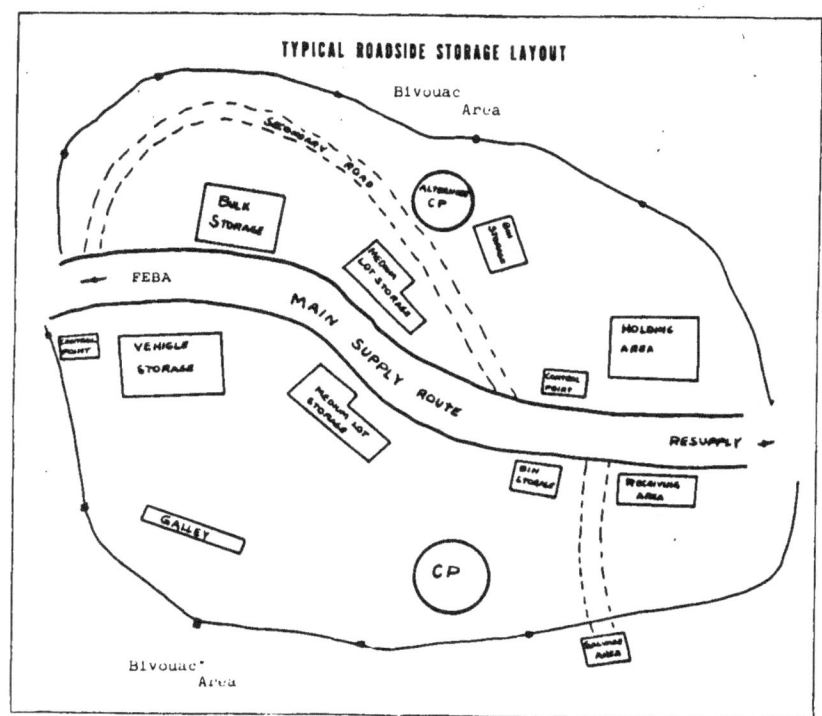

Figure 3-1.--Typical Roadside Dump.

Figure 3-1.--Typical Roadside Dump.

MARINE CORPS WAREHOUSING MANUAL

MARINE CORPS WAREHOUSING MANUAL

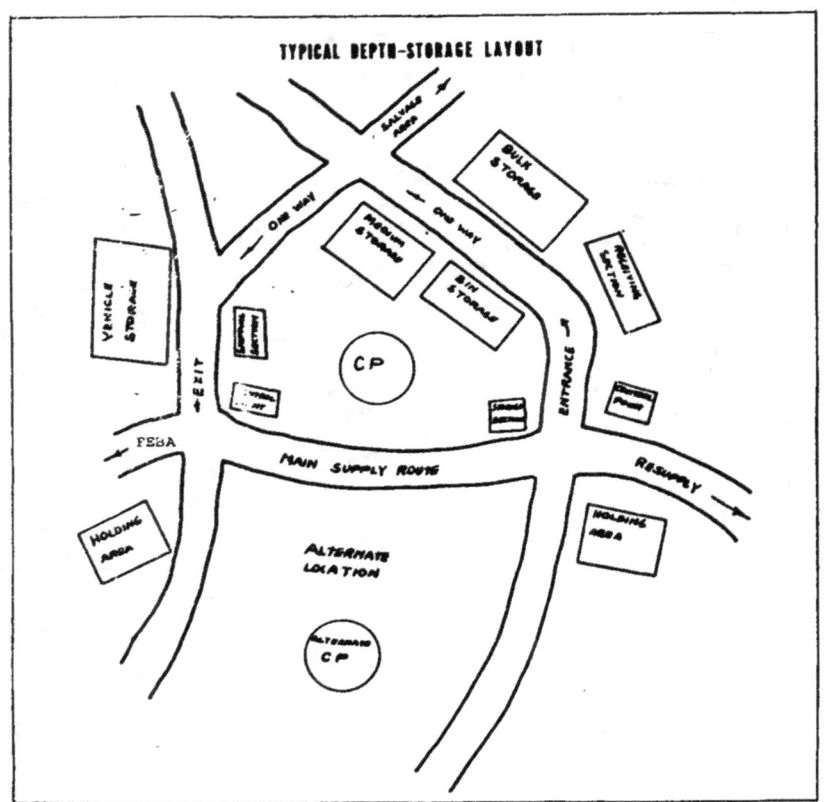

Figure 3-2.--Typical Depth-Storage Dump.

Figure 3-2.--Typical Depth-Storage Dump.

MARINE CORPS WAREHOUSING MANUAL

CHAPTER 4

REPORTS

	PARAGRAPH	PAGE
STORAGE SPACE MANAGEMENT REPORTING	4000	4-3
ACTIVITIES REQUIRED TO SUBMIT REPORTS	4001	4-3
STORAGE UNIT REPORT (NAVSUP FORM 605)	4002	4-4

FIGURE

| 4-1 | STORAGE UNIT REPORT | 4-6 |

MARINE CORPS WAREHOUSING MANUAL

CHAPTER 4

REPORTS

4000.   **STORAGE SPACE MANAGEMENT REPORTING**

1. **General Information**. The basic principles of storage space control and reporting are contained in DOD 4145.19-R-1.

2. **Reporting Instructions**. Storage Space Management Reports (Report Control Symbol DD-4450-02) will be prepared as directed in NavSupInst 4450.22. This will satisfy the Storage Space Management Report (DD Form 805) required by a DoD directive in the 4145 series. Navsupinst 4450.22 provides specific directions to complete the Storage Space Management Report, Navy Format/Worksheet, or DD Form 805.

3. **Other Information**

    a. The buildings/facilities to be included in storage space reporting are defined within category codes and building designations. These codes and designations are controlled by the CMC (LF). Category codes are assigned to types of facilities and are published in NAVFAC Pub's P-72 and P-80.

    b. Activities are encouraged to continually review DD Form 805 to ensure that the space reported does not include storage facilities being used for organic requirements. The following category code is provided in this connection:

    Category Code 441.12, General Storage Air/Ground Organic Units. This category includes general purpose storage facilities assigned to Marine Corps bases, air installations, and FMF units for organic requirements, to include division/wing, battalion/group, and company/squadron storage areas; base property storage/issue points maintenance facility storage areas; special services storerooms, base shipping, and receiving functions; and any other organic storage requirements. This facility category code is excluded from the Storage Space Management Report.

4001. <u>ACTIVITIES REQUIRED TO SUBMIT REPORTS</u>. The following
activities shall submit reports:

Marine Corps Logistics Base, Albany, Georgia

Marine Corps Logistics Base, Barstow, California

Marine Corps Base, Camp Pendleton, California

Marine Corps Base, Camp Lejeune, North Carolina

Marine Corps Base, Camp S. D. Butler, Okinawa

Marine Corps Base, Camp H. M. Smith, Hawaii

Marine Corps Base, Quantico, Virginia

Marine Corps Air-Ground Combat Center, Twentynine
Palms, California

Marine Corps Recruit Depot (Eastern Recruiting Region),
Parris Island, South Carolina

Marine Corps Recruit Depot (Western Recruiting Region),
San Diego, California

Marine Corps Air Station, Cherry Point, North Carolina

Marine Corps Air Station, Beaufort, South Carolina

Marine Corps Air Station, Quantico, Virginia

Marine Corps Air Station, El Toro, California

Marine Corps Air Station Tustin, California

Marine Corps Air Station, Yuma, Arizona

Marine Corps Air Station, Kaneohe Bay, Hawaii

Marine Corps Air Station, Iwakuni, Japan

4002.   STORAGE UNIT REPORT (NAVSUP FORM 605)

1. <u>General Information</u>. The Individual Storage Unit Report

(NAVSUP Form 605) is a one-time or change-in-situation report. It is used to report those storage and warehouse facilities, including all covered and open storage units, at a Marine Corps installation. (Report Symbol DD-4450-03 has been assigned to this report.) (See figure 4-1.) When preparation of NAVSUP Form 605 is necessary, it shall be prepared in an original and one copy and submitted to the CMC (LPP). When changes occur in a storage unit, either by structural alteration or diversion of warehouse space to another use, a revised NAVSUP Form 605 shall be included with the first DD Form 805 submitted subsequent to such alteration or diversion. However, when a storage unit is approved for disposition which ultimately results in the loss of the storage unit, or when the entire area for storage operations is vacated within nonwarehouse

space, such changes may be explained in the "Remarks" section of Storage Space Management Report, listing each unit involved.

2. Preparation of NAVSUP Form 605

    a. General Information. Each warehouse, shed, igloo, magazine, and/or improved storage area plot shall be considered as an individual storage unit. A multistory building shall be considered as one individual storage unit. Permanent buildings originally designed for, or converted to, warehouse space shall be reported regardless of cognizance, tenancy, or utilization. In one warehouse space, only that portion assigned to storage operation shall be reported as a storage unit.

    b. Detailed Instructions. For detailed instructions for preparing NAVSUP Form 605, see figure 4-1.

MARINE CORPS WAREHOUSING MANUAL

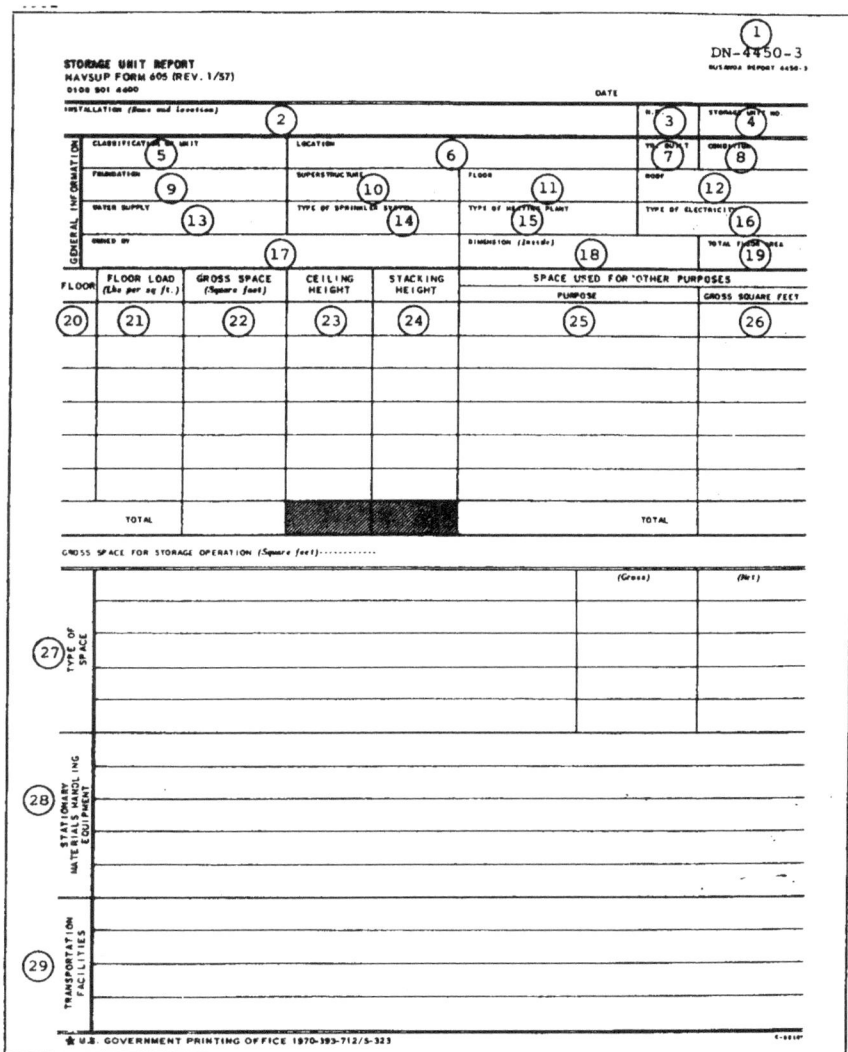

Figure 4-1.   Storage Unit Report.

Figure 4-1.--Storage Unit Report.

Legend

1. <u>Report Symbol</u>. In the upper right-hand corner, on all reports, Marine Corps Report Symbol "DD-4450-3" shall appear directly above "BUSANDA Report 4450-3."

2. <u>Installation</u>. Enter the complete name of the Marine Corps activity.

3. <u>N.D</u>. Enter the appropriate naval district.

4. <u>Storage Unit No</u>. Enter the official building number of the storage unit.

5. <u>Classification of Unit</u>. Enter information as to wether the unit is a warehouse, nonwarehouse (type structure), or open improved area.

6. <u>Location</u>. Enter the word "station."

7. <u>Year Build</u>. Enter the year in which the construction of the unit was completed.

8. <u>Condition</u>. Enter information as to whether the condition of the unit is poor, fair, good, or excellent.

9. <u>Foundation</u>. Enter the type of material used in construction of the foundation; e.g., reinforced concrete, wood, etc.

10. <u>Superstructure</u>. Enter the type of material used in the construction; e.g., concrete, steel, wood, etc.

11. <u>Floor</u>. Enter the type of material used in the construction of the floor; e.g., wood, concrete, asphalt, etc.

12. <u>Roof</u>. Enter the type of material used in the construction of the roof; e.g., asbestos, shingling, composite strapping, etc.

13. <u>Water Supply</u>. Enter the source from which water is obtained. If water is not available, then enter "None."

14. <u>Type of Sprinkler System</u>. Enter information as to whether the system is wet or dry. If no sprinkler system is used, enter "none."

Figure 4-1.--Storage Unit Report--Continued.

Legend (contd)

15. Type of Heating Plant. Enter the type of heating plant utilized within the storage unit; e.g., hot air, steam, hot water, etc. Individual space heaters shall not be considered as heating plants, unless they provide heat for the storage unit.

16. Type of Electricity. Enter the type of electricity by voltage, a.c. or d.c., and the number of cycles; e.g., 120-220 volts, 60 cycles, a.c.

17. Owned By. Enter "Marine Corps-Owned."

18. Dimension (Inside)

    a. For covered space, enter the inside measurements between exterior walls. Do not deduct space for fire walls or others structural loss.

    b. For open improved space, enter the overall measurements of the open space. Do not deduct space for trackage or permanent roads.

19. Total Floor Area. Self-explanatory.

20. Floor. Enter the floor number.

21. Floor Load. Enter the authorized floor load capacity in pounds per square feet.

22. Gross Space. Through utilization of internal measurements, enter the gross square feet of space available for storage operations on each floor.

23. Ceiling Height. Enter the maximum ceiling height for each floor. For buildings with variable ceiling heights, enter each section separately.

24. Stacking Height. Enter the maximum height to which supplies may be stored, compatible with fire regulations and good warehousing practices.

25. Space Used for Other Purposes. Enter a brief description of the function for which the space will be used and the gross square feet involved.

Figure 4-1.--Storage Unit Report--Continued.

MARINE CORPS WAREHOUSING MANUAL

Legend (contd)

26. Gross Square Feet for Storage Operation. Enter the gross
    square feet of space which is used for any operation
    concerning storage or storage support. This figure shall be
    reflected in, and equal to, the totals reported on DD
    Form 805, line 7, columns b through n.

27. Type of Space. Enter information as to whether the space is
    general, heavy-duty, heated, unheated, controlled
    humidity, chill, freeze, etc. Enter the type of material
    used in the surfacing of an open improved area.

28. Stationary Materials Handling Equipment. Enter the total
    number of stationary materials handling equipment, by type
    and operation, located at each storage unit.

29. Transportation Facilities. Enter the type of transportation
    facility available or the capacity, location, or loading
    levels of the facility.

Figure 4-1.--Storage Unit Report--Continued.

MARINE CORPS WAREHOUSING MANUAL

CHAPTER 5

WAREHOUSING REFERENCES

	PARAGRAPH	PAGE
GENERAL INFORMATION	5000	5-3
AVAILABILITY OF REFERENCES	5001	5-3
LIST OF WAREHOUSING REFERENCES	5002	5-3

MARINE CORPS WAREHOUSING MANUAL

CHAPTER 5

WAREHOUSING REFERENCES

5000. <u>GENERAL INFORMATION</u>. The references in this chapter are a partial listing of <u>basic</u> warehousing documents (technical, administrative, operational, training, and procedural in nature) and are presented here as a ready reference. The listing will prove helpful to personnel involved in other elements of supply and distribution on which warehousing and storage have an impact or interface (i.e., procurement, technical, stock management, transportation, and packaging).

5001. <u>AVAILABILITY OF REFERENCES</u>. Activity allowances have been established for only a limited number of the publications listed in this chapter. It is recognized that the limited distribution allowance may not be adequate and that many activities now engaged in warehousing and storage are not covered by established distribution allowances. Nevertheless, these and other publications, as may be listed in DOD 4120.3-M and other services indexes, are available as follows:

1. <u>Military Specifications and Standards</u>. Refer to MCO 4120.5.

2. <u>Marine Corps Letter and P-Type Directives and Joint Services Publications</u>. Refer to MCO P5600.31, section III.

3. <u>Other Services Publications</u>. Refer to MCO P5600.31, section III.

5002. <u>LIST OF WAREHOUSING REFERENCES</u>. It is emphasized that the following listing of warehousing publications is limited to basic technical and procedural type documents.

1. Department of Defense Publications

Regulation	Subject
DoD 4145.19-R-1	Storage and Materials Handling

Manual	Subject
DoD 4140.27-M	Identification, Control and Utilization of Shelf Life Items

2. Department of the Navy Publications

NAVSUPINST	Subject
4450.22	Storage Space Management Reporting System

NAVSUP	Subject
P-529	Warehouse Modernization and Layout Planning Guide

NAVFAC	Subject
P-72	Facilities Category Codes
P-80	Facility Planning Criteria for Navy and Marine Corps Shore Installations

3. Marine Corps Publications

MCO Number	Subject
MCO P4030.36	Packaging Manual
MCO 4450.10	Storage and Warehousing Operations and Equipment Modernization Planning and Programming

MCO P4450.12   Storage and Handling of
                      Hazardous Material

FMFM 4-1   Combat Service Support
                      Operations

UM 4400-120   Asset Tracking for Logistics
                      and Supply Systems

UM 4400-171   Warehouse Support System

MARINE CORPS WAREHOUSING MANUAL

APPENDIX A

GLOSSARY OF TERMS

1. <u>General Information</u>. DoD 4145.19-R-1, chapter I, section 2, contains a glossary of terms, the majority of which are contained herein. The terms contained in DOD 4145.19-R-1, chapter I, section 2, shall be used, unless the terms in question are further defined herein.

2. <u>Definitions</u>. The terms defined in the following are used within the context of this Manual:

<u>Aisles</u>. Any passageway in storage areas.

<u>Cross-Servicing</u>. Services performed and/or materiel, supplies, equipment, or space furnished by one DOD component to another DOD component or Federal Government agency.

<u>Disestablish</u>. To discontinue operation of a function or mission.

<u>Diversion</u>. To change identity of storage space through alteration or construction.

<u>DoD Component</u>. A military service or agency of the DoD.

<u>Exercising</u>. The lubrication of equipment in storage through a

self-contained power supply or through a remote/external power source.

Inactive. To temporarily discontinue use of a facility.

Inspection, Cyclic. A periodic inspection of materiel for the purpose of detecting the presence of corrosion, mutilated wrappings, container fatigue, and/or marking deficiencies.

Item, Critical. An item which, through deterioration or contamination, would cause premature failure or malfunction of an item, excessive repair or overhaul costs, or unsafe or hazardous operating conditions.

Item, Line. A separate item of supply on a transaction document.

Logistics Marking and Reading Symbology (LOGMARS). A scanning technology that utilizes bar-coded labels on items being shipped, inventoried, or warehoused in the supply system.

Measurement Ton. A quantity of materiel which has a volume of 40 cubic feet, regardless of weight.

MARINE CORPS WAREHOUSING MANUAL

Military Construction. Construction in excess of $300,000 for a single project or location.

Operation and Maintenance, Marine Corps, Repair and Minor Construction Projects. Repair projects having no funding limit but authority approval levels of $300,000 per project at the activity level and up to $3 million at the Headquarters, Marine Corps level. Projects above $3 million may require Secretary of the Navy approval. Minor construction projects have a $100,000 limit at the activity level and $300,000 at the CMC level.

Packaging. The process and procedures used to protect material from deterioration and/or damage. Includes cleaning, drying, preserving, packing, marking, and utilization. (See packing and preservation.)

Packing. Assembly of items into a unit, intermediate, or exterior pack with necessary blocking, bracing, cushioning, weatherproofing, reinforcement, and marking.

Parcel Post. A package that is either shipped or received by the U.S. Postal Service.

Potential Stacking Height. The maximum height to which supplies can be stored, compatible with good warehousing practices.

Preservation. The application of adequate preservative measures to prevent deterioration of items resulting from exposure to atmospheric conditions during storage and shipment.

Preservation, Cyclic. The represervation, repacking, and/or repackaging of materiel.

Short Ton. A quantity of materiel that has a gross weight of 2,000 pounds, regardless of volume.

Space Assignment. Space within an installation designated specifically for storage purposes.

Space, Chill. Refrigerated warehouse area in which the temperature can be controlled between 30OF./0 C. and 50OF./10OC.

Space, Controlled Humidity Nonwarehouse. Nonwarehouse space equipped with humidity control equipment, including controlled humidity dry tanks, whether or not such equipment is in operation.

Space, Controlled Humidity Warehouse. Space in a warehouse equipped with humidity control equipment.

Space, Covered. Area within any roofed structure.

A-2

MARINE CORPS WAREHOUSING MANUAL

Space, Flammable. Warehouse area which has been designed for the storage of highly flammable material.

Space, Freeze. Refrigerated warehouse space in which the temperature can be controlled below a level of 32OF./0 C.

Space, General Purpose. Warehouse space, other than controlled humidity, flammable, and refrigerated warehouse space.

Space, Licensed or Permitted. Space used under a right of exclusive use granted by the licenser. A privilege, revokable at will, to use the property of the licenser for a specified purpose and period of time.

Space, Magazine, Above Ground. An area within a warehouse-type structure designated for storage of ammunition and explosives.

Space, Nonwarehouse. Any covered area, other than actual designated warehouse space, which is assigned for storage purposes. All storage space that is located in buildings which are listed on the plant account record as having been built for purposes other than storage. Buildings, such as barracks, drill halls, hangars, quonset huts, or similar buildings when assigned or designated as storage facilities.

Space, Outleased. Storage space leased to a private or commercial industrial enterprise for which rent is paid by the leasee.

Space, Standby. Storage space contained in open, improved areas which is not required to support the installation's mission or completely empty, covered structures which have been secured.

Space, Support. That area which is used for preservation and packaging, assembly, packing, crating, container manufacturing, receiving, shipping, inspection and identification, administrative storage offices, employee rest areas, toolrooms, timeclock areas, battery charging stations, and other similar support functions.

Structure Loss Space. Space not usable for storage because of construction features or physical characteristics of a warehouse facility or improved open storage area.

Test, Operational. A test by which technically qualified personnel determine whether materiel is functionally and operationally ready for issue.

Transfer Operation. An operation whereby materiel is unloaded from one transportation vehicle when the materiel is concurrently received and shipped without an intermediate storage period other than that holding incident to the transfer operation.

MARINE CORPS WAREHOUSING MANUAL

Unspecified Minor Construction (UMC). Any construction project having a funded cost greater than $300 but less than $1.5 million which demands remedy sooner than would be possible if delayed for authorization and funding through the regular MILCON program. UMC projects will be funded through the military construction appropriation.

Warehouse Facility. The structure in which the physical function relating to receipt, storage, and issue of supplies is performed.

Warehousing Services. The operations within a warehouse facility including, but not limited to, the receipt, storage, PP&P, and issue of supplies.

Warehouse Support System. A system using LOGMARS technology to automate the basic warehouse functions of location determination, location surveillance/verification, and physical inventory.

MARINE CORPS WAREHOUSING MANUAL

APPENDIX B

STORAGE LOCATION EXAMPLES

FIGURE   PAGE

B-1   AREA EXAMPLES B-3

B-2   STATION EXAMPLES B-4

B-3   AISLE AND SEGMENT BULK STORAGE B-5

B-4   AISLE AND SEGMENT BIN STORAGE B-6

B-5   SEGMENT-LEVEL-COMPARTMENT BIN
         STORAGE B-7

B-6   SEGMENT-LEVEL-COMPARTMENT DIVIDED
       BIN STORAGE B-8

B-7   SEGMENT-LEVEL-COMPARTMENT ROTO
       BIN STORAGE B-9

B-8   MARKINGS FOR BIN STORAGE UNIT B-10

B-1

MARINE CORPS WAREHOUSING MANUAL

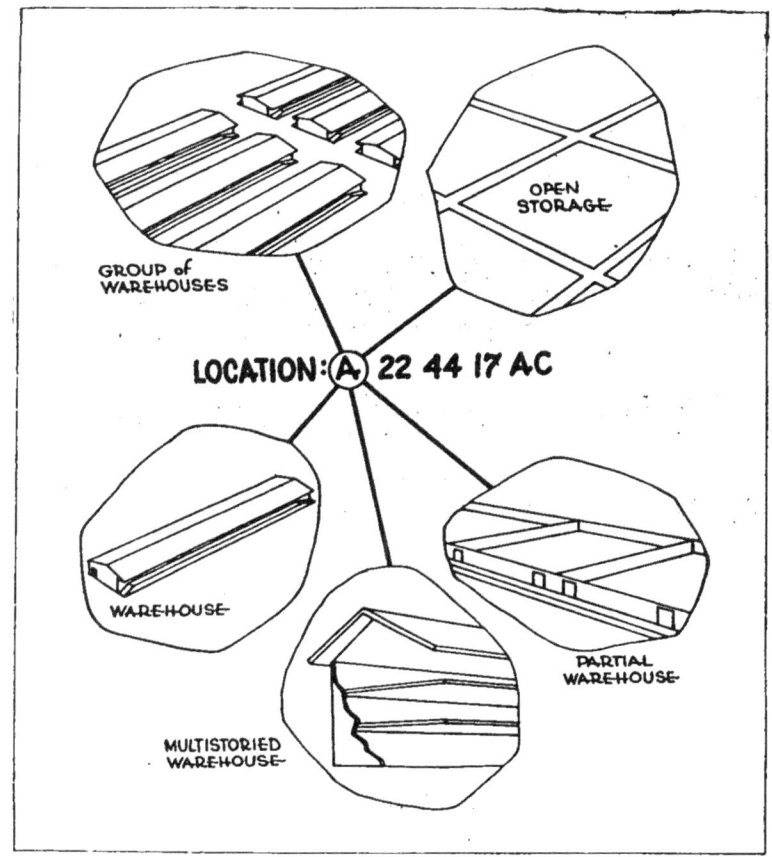

Figure B-1.--Area Examples.

Figure B-1.--Area Examples

B-3

MARINE CORPS WAREHOUSING MANUAL

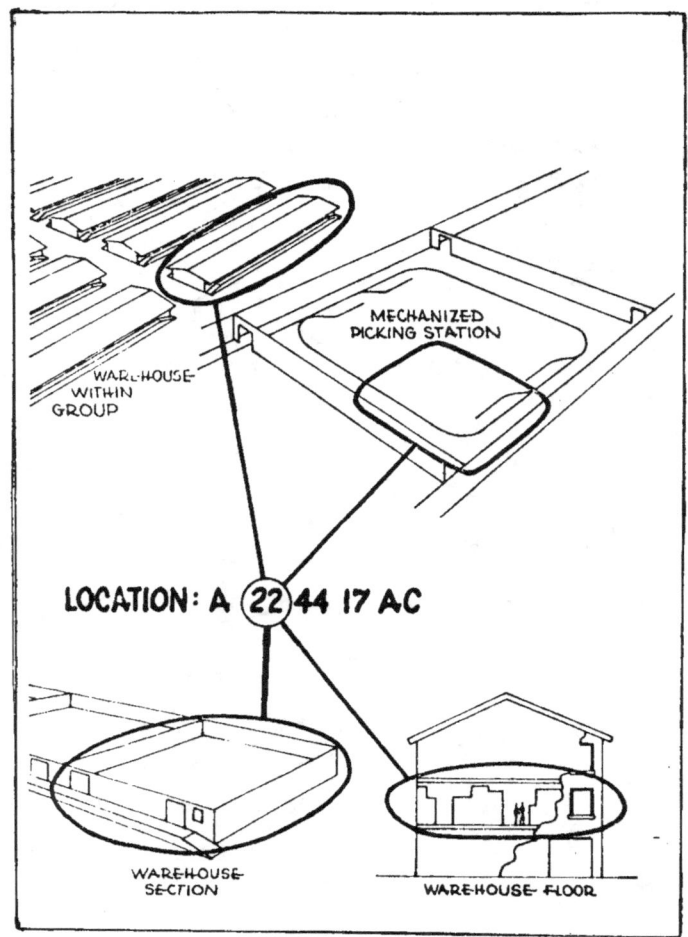

Figure B-2.--Station Examples.

Figure B-2.--Station Examples

B-4

MARINE CORPS WAREHOUSING MANUAL

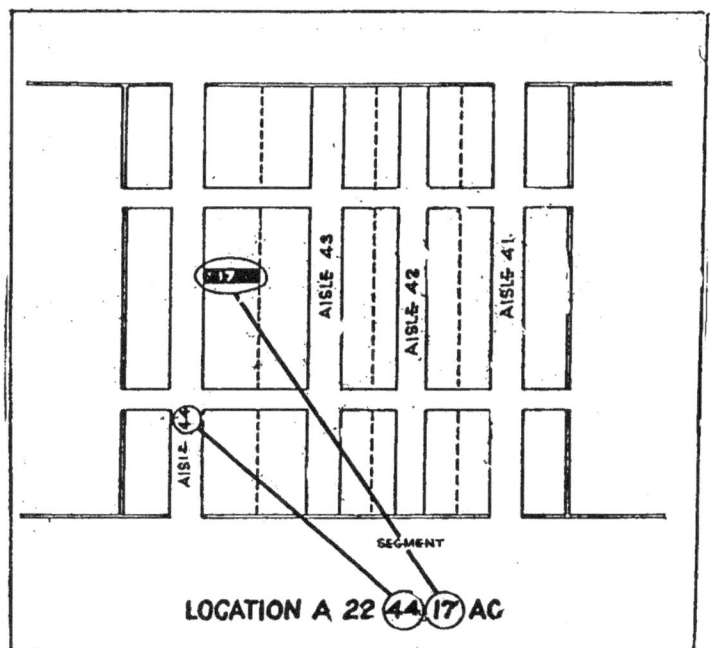

Figure B-3.--Aisle and Segment Bulk Storage.

Figure B-3.--Aisle and Segment Storage.

MARINE CORPS WAREHOUSING MANUAL

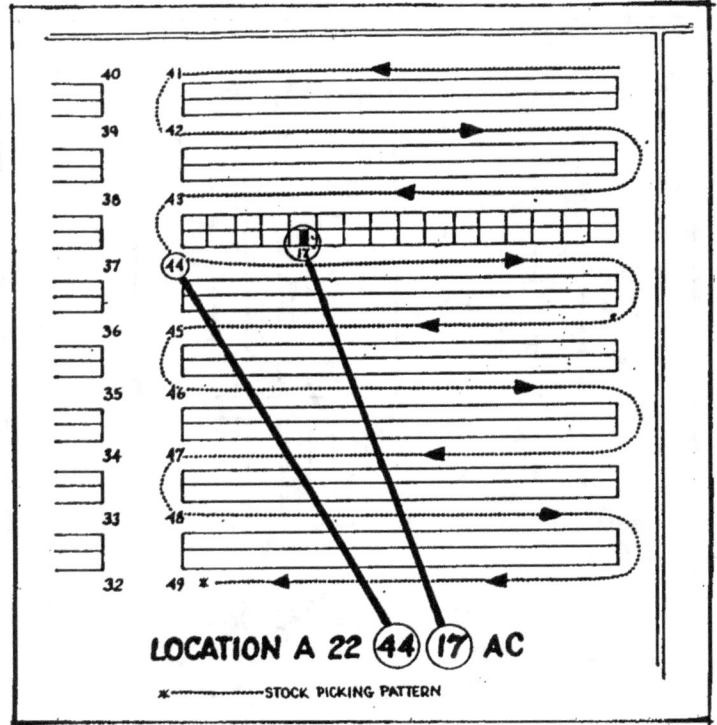

Figure B-4.--Aisle and Segment Bin Storage.

Figure B-4.--Aisle and Segment Bin Storage.

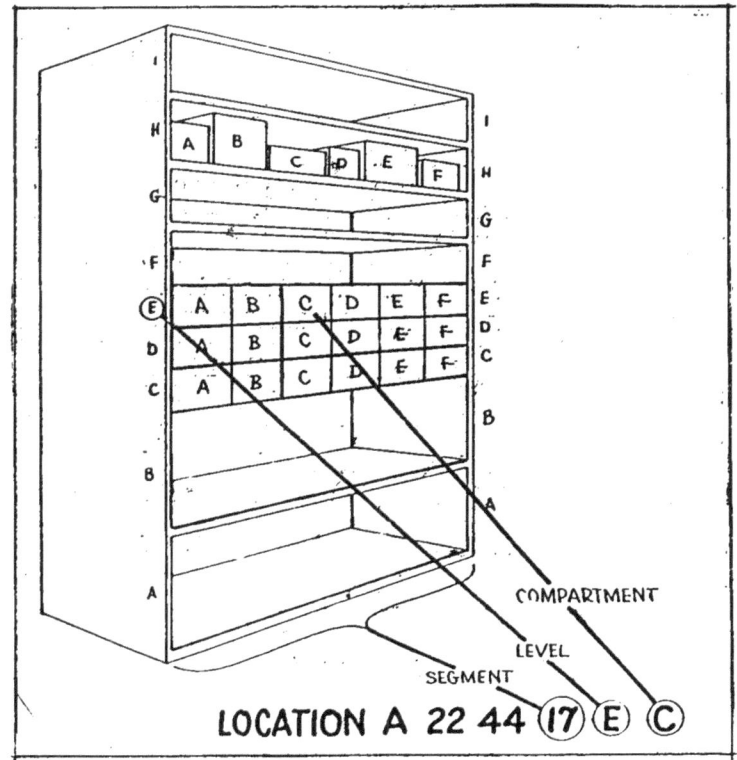

LOCATION A 22 44 (17)(E)(C)

Figure B-5.--Segment-Level-Compartment Bin Storage.

Figure B-5.--Segment-Level-Compartment Bin Storage.

B-7

MARINE CORPS WAREHOUSING MANUAL

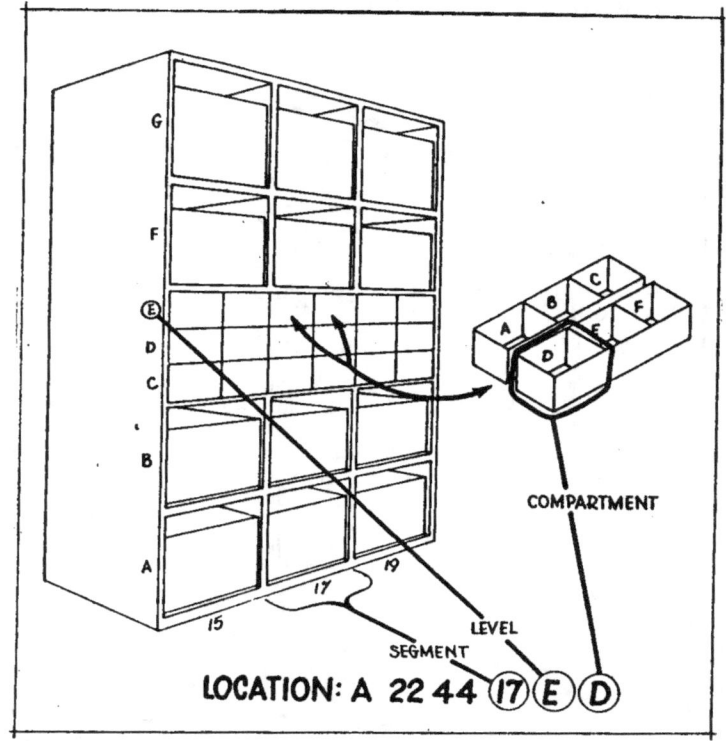

Figure B-6.--Segment-Level-Compartment Divided Bin Storage.

Figure B-6.--Segment-Level-Compartment Divided Bin Storage.

MARINE CORPS WAREHOUSING MANUAL

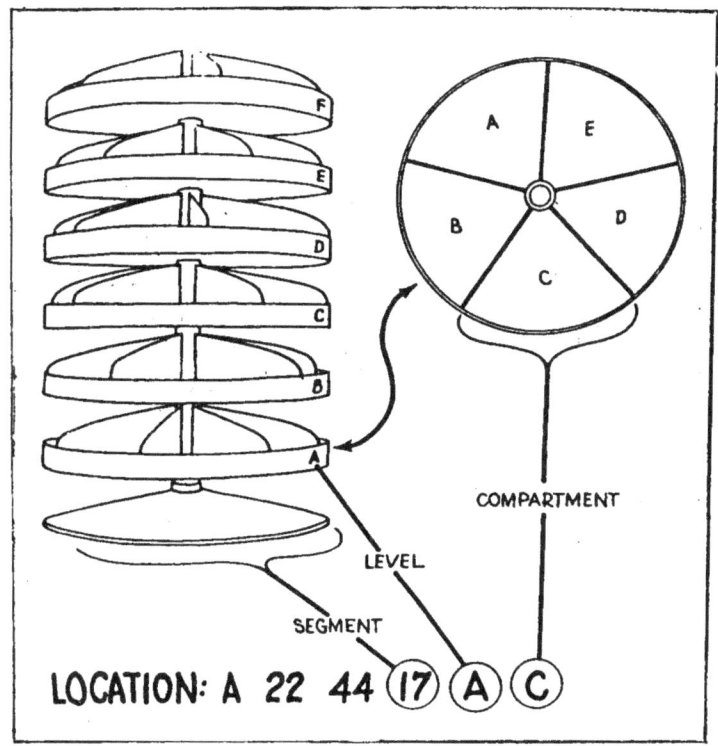

LOCATION: A 22 44 ⑰ Ⓐ Ⓒ

Figure B-7.--Segment-Level-Compartment Roto Bin Storage.

Figure B-7.--Segment-Level-Compartment Roto Bin Storage.

B-9

MARINE CORPS WAREHOUSING MANUAL

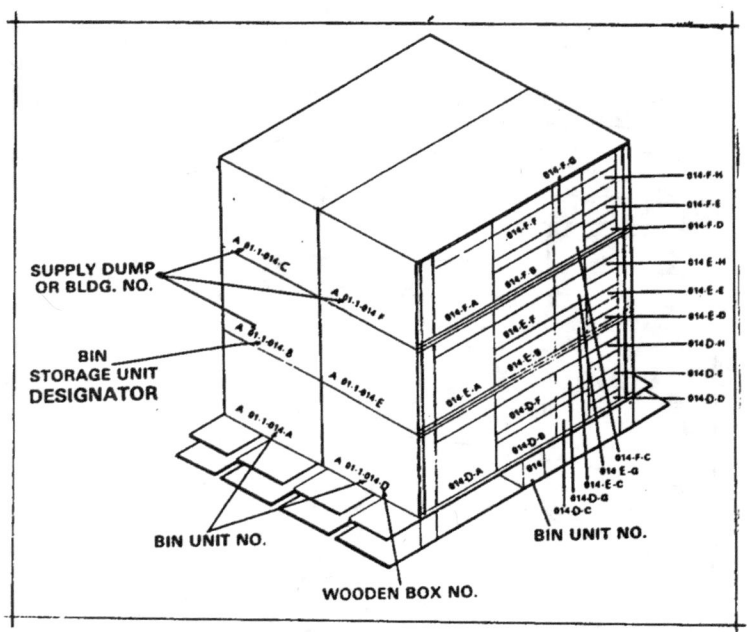

Figure B-8.--Markings for Bin Storage Unit.

Figure B-8.--Markings for Bin Storage Unit.

MARINE CORPS WAREHOUSING MANUAL

APPENDIX C

STORAGE CONTAINERS

FIGURE   PAGE

C-1   WOODEN BOX AND INSERTS C-3

C-2   PALLET AND PALLET BOX C-3

C-3   BULK STORAGE UNITS C-4

C-4   QUADCON C-5

C-5   PALCON C-6

MARINE CORPS WAREHOUSING MANUAL

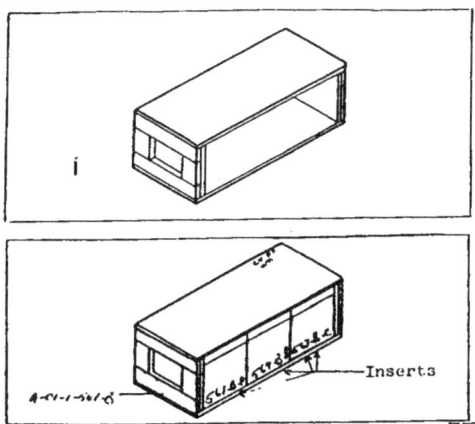

Figure C-1.--Wooden Box and Inserts.

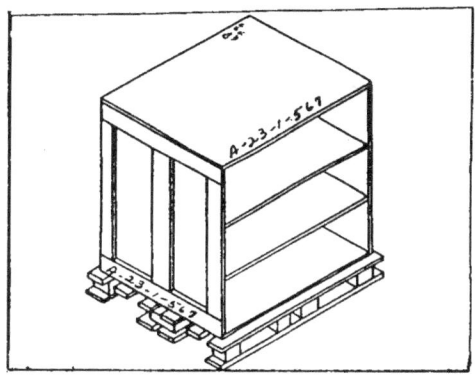

Figure C-2.--Pallet and Pallet Box.

Figure C-2.--Pallet and Pallet Box.

C-3

MARINE CORPS WAREHOUSING MANUAL

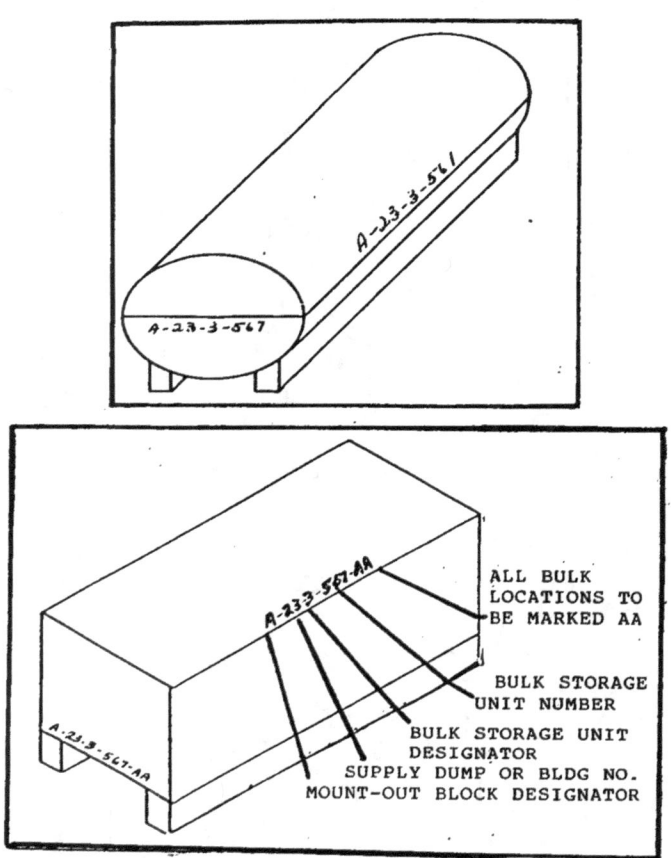

ALL BULK
LOCATIONS TO
BE MARKED AA

BULK STORAGE
UNIT NUMBER

BULK STORAGE UNIT
DESIGNATOR
SUPPLY DUMP OR BLDG NO.
MOUNT-OUT BLOCK DESIGNATOR

Figure C-3.--Bulk Storage Units.

C-4

Figure C-3.--Bulk Storage Units.

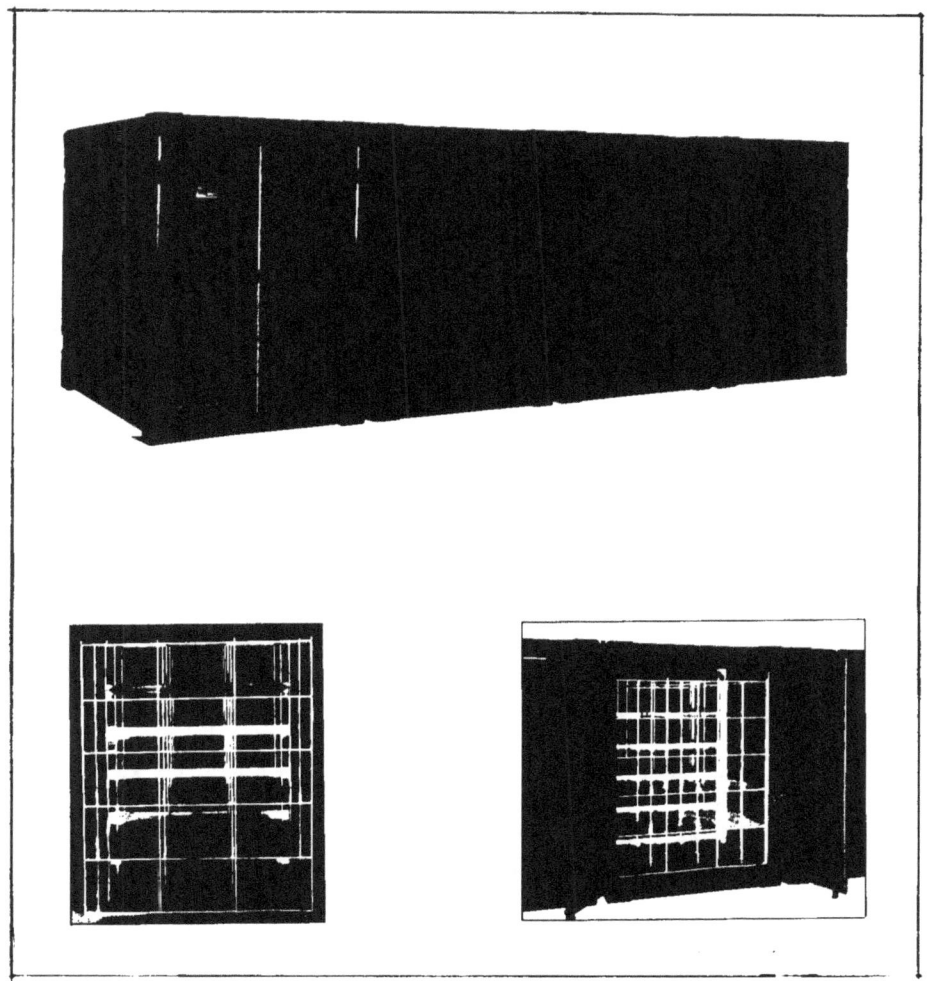

Figure C-4.--QUADCON.

Figure C-4.--QUADCON.

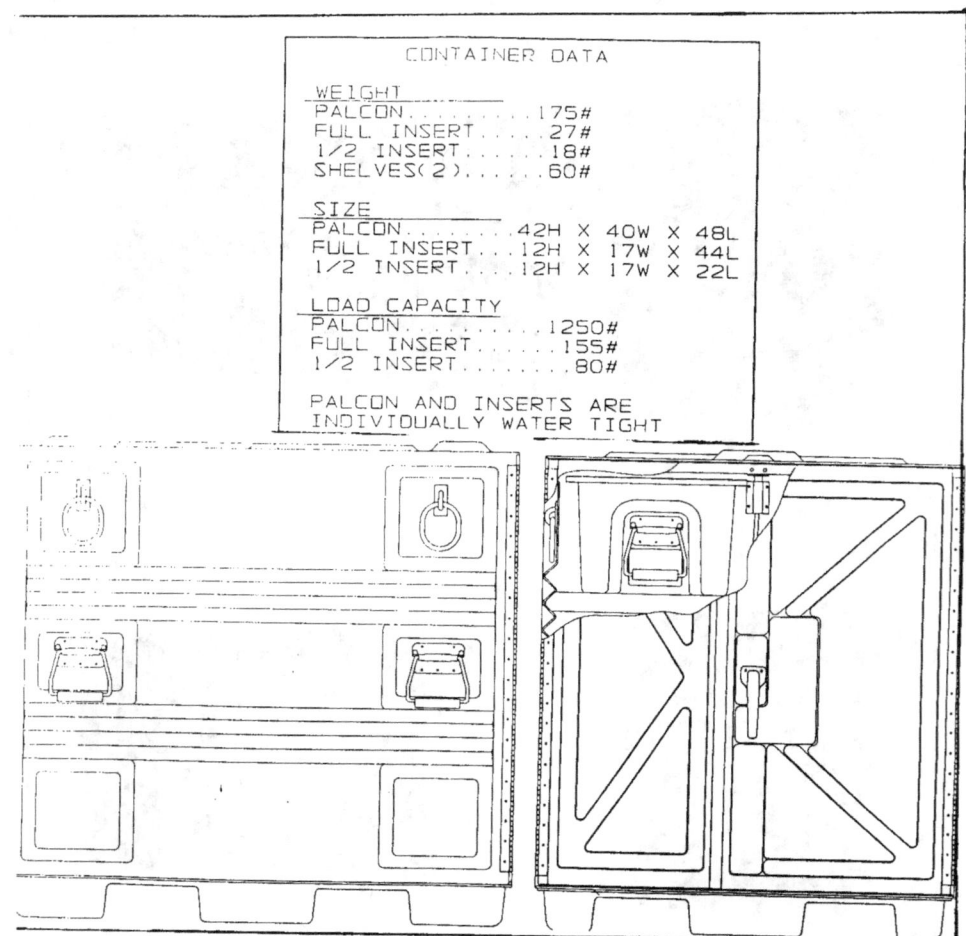

CONTAINER DATA

WEIGHT
PALCON.........175#
FULL INSERT.....27#
1/2 INSERT......18#
SHELVES(2)......60#

SIZE
PALCON.........42H X 40W X 48L
FULL INSERT...12H X 17W X 44L
1/2 INSERT....12H X 17W X 22L

LOAD CAPACITY
PALCON.........1250#
FULL INSERT......155#
1/2 INSERT........80#

PALCON AND INSERTS ARE
INDIVIDUALLY WATER TIGHT

Figure C-5.--PALCON.

Figure C-5.--PALCON.

MARINE CORPS WAREHOUSING MANUAL

APPENDIX D

ACRONYMS AND ABBREVIATIONS

CC	Card Column
CMC	Commandant of the Marine Corps
DIC	Document Identifier Code
DoD	Department of Defense
DoDAC	Department of Defense Ammunition Code
ECUC	Equipment End User Computer Equipment
FEBA	Forward Edge of the Battle Area
FMF	Fleet Marine Force
LOGMARS	Logistics Marking and Reading Symbology
MSR	Main Supply Route
NSN	National Stock Number
PP&P	Preservation, Packaging, and Packing
RASC	Regional Automated Services Center
SASSY	Supported Activities Supply System
TAMCN	Table of Authorized Materiel Control Number
UP&TT	Unit Personnel & Tonnage Table
WSS	Warehouse Support System